Your Government:
How It Works

The Drug
Enforcement
Administration

Meg Greene

Arthur M. Schlesinger, jr.
Senior Consulting Editor

Chelsea House Publishers
Philadelphia

CHELSEA HOUSE PUBLISHERS
Production Manager Pamela Loos
Art Director Sara Davis
Director of Photography Judy L. Hasday
Managing Editor James D. Gallagher
Senior Production Editor J. Christopher Higgins

Staff for THE DRUG ENFORCEMENT ADMINISTRATION
Project Editor/Publishing Coordinator Jim McAvoy
Associate Art Director Takeshi Takahashi
Series Designers Takeshi Takahashi, Keith Trego

The Chelsea House World Wide Web address is
http://www.chelseahouse.com

First Printing
1 3 5 7 9 8 6 4 2

Library of Congress Cataloging-in-Publication Data

Greene, Meg.
The Drug Enforcement Administration: your government—how it
works/Meg Greene.
  p. cm.
Includes bibliographical references and index.
ISBN 0-7910-5992-8
  1. United States. Drug Enforcement Administration—Juvenile
literature. 2. Narcotics, Control of—United States—
Juvenile literature. [1. United States. Drug Enforcement Administration. 2. Narcotics, Control of.] I. Title.

HV5825 .G6962 2000
353.3'7—dc21   00-034599

Contents

The Attorney General's Office

The Cabinet

The Central Intelligence Agency

The Drug Enforcement Administration

The Federal Bureau of Investigation

The History of the Democratic Party

The History of the Republican Party

The History of Third Parties

The House of Representatives

How a Bill Is Passed

How to Become an Elected Official

The Impeachment Process

The Internal Revenue Service

The Presidency

The Secretary of State

The Senate

The Speaker of the House of Representatives

The Supreme Court

The U.S. Armed Forces

The U.S. Constitution

The U.S. Secret Service

The Vice Presidency

Introduction

Government: Crises of Confidence

Arthur M. Schlesinger, jr.

FROM THE START, Americans have regarded their government with a mixture of reliance and mistrust. The men who founded the republic understood the importance of government. "If men were angels," observed the 51st Federalist Paper, "no government would be necessary." But men are not angels. Because human beings are subject to wicked as well as to noble impulses, government was deemed essential to assure freedom and order.

The American revolutionaries, however, also knew that government could become a source of injury and oppression. The men who gathered in Philadelphia in 1787 to write the Constitution therefore had two purposes in mind: They wanted to establish a strong central authority and to limit that central authority's capacity to abuse its power.

To prevent the abuse of power, the Founding Fathers wrote two basic principles into the Constitution. The principle of federalism divided power between the state governments and the central authority. The principle of the separation of powers subdivided the central authority itself into three branches—the executive, the legislative, and the judiciary—so that "each may be a check on the other."

YOUR GOVERNMENT: HOW IT WORKS examines some of the major parts of that central authority, the federal government. It explains how various officials, agencies, and departments operate and explores the political organizations that have grown up to serve the needs of government.

Introduction

The federal government as presented in the Constitution was more an idealistic construct than a practical administrative structure. It was barely functional when it came into being.

This was especially true of the executive branch. The Constitution did not describe the executive branch in any detail. After vesting executive power in the president, it assumed the existence of "executive departments" without specifying what these departments should be. Congress began defining their functions in 1789 by creating the Departments of State, Treasury, and War.

President Washington, assisted by Secretary of the Treasury Alexander Hamilton, equipped the infant republic with a working administrative structure. Congress also continued that process by creating more executive departments as they were needed.

Throughout the 19th century, the number of federal government workers increased at a consistently faster rate than did the population. Increasing concerns about the politicization of public service led to efforts—bitterly opposed by politicians—to reform it in the latter part of the century.

The 20th century saw considerable expansion of the federal establishment. More importantly, it saw growing impatience with bureaucracy in society as a whole.

The Great Depression during the 1930s confronted the nation with its greatest crisis since the Civil War. Under Franklin Roosevelt, the New Deal reshaped the federal government, assigning it a variety of new responsibilities and greatly expanding its regulatory functions. By 1940, the number of federal workers passed the 1 million mark.

Critics complained of big government and bureaucracy. Business owners resented federal regulation. Conservatives worried about the impact of paternalistic government on self-reliance, on community responsibility, and on economic and personal freedom.

When the United States entered World War II in 1941, government agencies focused their energies on supporting the war effort. By the end of World War II, federal civilian employment had risen to 3.8 million. With peace, the federal establishment declined to around 2 million in 1950. Then growth resumed, reaching 2.8 million by the 1980s.

A large part of this growth was the result of the national government assuming new functions such as: affirmative action in civil rights, environmental protection, and safety and health in the workplace.

Some critics became convinced that the national government was a steadily growing behemoth swallowing up the liberties of the people. The 1980s brought new intensity to the debate about government growth. Foes of Washington bureaucrats preferred local government, feeling it more responsive to popular needs.

But local government is characteristically the government of the locally powerful. Historically, the locally powerless have often won their human and constitutional rights by appealing to the national government. The national government has defended racial justice against local bigotry, upheld the Bill of Rights against local vigilantism, and protected natural resources from local greed. It has civilized industry and secured the rights of labor organizations. Had the states' rights creed prevailed, perhaps slavery would still exist in the United States.

Americans are still of two minds. When pollsters ask large, spacious questions—Do you think government has become too involved in your lives? Do you think government should stop regulating business?—a sizable majority opposes big government. But when asked specific questions about the practical work of government—Do you favor Social Security? Unemployment compensation? Medicare? Health and safety standards in factories? Environmental protection?—a sizable majority approves of intervention.

We do not like bureaucracy, but we cannot live without it. We need its genius for organizing the intricate details of our daily lives. Without bureaucracy, modern society would collapse. It would be impossible to run any of the large public and private organizations we depend on without bureaucracy's division of labor and hierarchy of authority. The challenge is to keep these necessary structures of our civilization flexible, efficient, and capable of innovation.

More than 200 years after the drafting of the Constitution, Americans still rely on government but also mistrust it. These attitudes continue to serve us well. What we mistrust, we are more likely to monitor. And government needs our constant attention if it is to avoid inefficiency, incompetence, and arbitrariness. Without our informed participation, it cannot serve us individually or help us as a people to attain the lofty goals of the Founding Fathers.

A young man is arrested for drug possession in a sting operation organized by the Drug Enforcement Administration. The DEA is responsible for overseeing the United States' efforts to end the illegal trafficking of drugs.

CHAPTER 1

A New Agency Is Born

BY THE SUMMER OF 1973 it was clear that something had to be done. For some years, the sale and use of illegal drugs in the United States had risen at an alarming rate. Baby boomers (men and women born between 1946 and 1964) were increasingly experimenting with drugs like marijuana. **Hallucinogens** such as lysergic acid diethylamide, or LSD, once used only in government experiments, were being sold on street corners and college campuses across the nation. The overworked and understaffed drug enforcement system was already combating the sale and use of illegal drugs. But the illegal sale of prescription drugs like amphetamines ("uppers") and barbiturates ("downers") was also on the rise. These **narcotics** were often stolen from hospitals and pharmacies and then illegally sold.

The federal government had until this point relied on the Bureau of Narcotics, a division of the Treasury Department, and the Bureau of Drug Abuse Control, which operated under the Food and Drug

Administration, to halt the illegal sale and use of drugs. To coordinate the efforts of these formerly independent agencies, President Lyndon B. Johnson combined them into a single agency in 1967. It was named the Bureau of Narcotics and Dangerous Drugs, or the BNDD. Johnson shifted control of this new agency from the Treasury Department to the Department of Justice. The BNDD fell under the direct supervision of the attorney general, the chief law enforcement officer in the United States.

Meanwhile, Congress had been busy enacting some important antidrug laws. In 1970, the Comprehensive Drug Abuse Prevention and Control Act became the law of the land. Known as the Controlled Substances Act, this legislation formed the basis for all future government policies in the war on drugs. In essence, the law set guidelines for the distribution of more than 20,000 types of drugs. And it set penalties for those convicted of illegally making, selling, or using them.

The law was composed of three parts: Title I, Title II, and Title III. Title I outlined the "mission statement," or purpose, of the law. According to Congress, the Controlled Substances Act was designed to regulate the **trafficking** in any drug considered dangerous. By focusing on what was called a "closed distribution system," drug enforcement agencies agreed to "monitor the manufacture, import, export, and distribution of all dangerous drugs and their raw materials." In other words, these agencies were given the power to regulate any activity involving dangerous drugs, whether it was the manufacture of an illegal substance or the sale of prescription drugs in the United States and abroad.

Titles II and III explained how the act was to be enforced. Through a system of classifications, or "schedules," the Controlled Substances Act categorized each drug covered by the law. Each of the 20,000 drugs classified

A DEA agent crouches next to 5,137 pounds of seized cocaine on a dock in Miami, Florida. Cocaine is considered a Schedule II drug due to its occasional use for medicinal purposes.

under the act fell into one of five schedules. To be pegged as "dangerous," drugs were evaluated according to three criteria. First, what degree of health risk did a drug pose? Was abuse of a drug likely to result in illness or death? Was the drug psychologically or physically addictive, or both? Second, what was the likelihood that persons would abuse a drug? Was the supply plentiful? Could a drug be made with relative ease and at a low cost? Was a drug inexpensive to purchase? Third, did a drug, if properly given under the care of a physician, have a legitimate medical use?

According to these criteria, the drugs listed on Schedule I, such as heroin, LSD, marijuana, peyote, and mescaline, were the most dangerous. They were seen to have no medicinal value and were considered highly addictive. Schedule II drugs were no less dangerous, but they did have some medical uses. Still, if improperly given or if abused, they could cause illness or death. The law also classified them as highly addictive. Drugs categorized on Schedule II included opium, cocaine, morphine, and methamphetamine.

Schedules III, IV, and V contained drugs that, although having the potential to be addictive, were not as dangerous as those found on Schedules I or II. Schedule III and IV drugs contained small amounts of narcotic and as such were available only by prescription. Some examples of these types were paregoric, which was placed on Schedule III, and Valium, a popular **antidepressant,** which was listed as a Schedule IV substance. Schedule V drugs were those containing small amounts of opium or codeine, a substance often found in cough suppressants. Unlike Schedule III and IV drugs, however, Schedule V drugs could readily be obtained without a doctor's prescription.

The law provided that new drugs could be added to the existing lists at any time. Drugs might also be removed from one schedule and placed on another if medical research warranted a change. Research, for example, showed amphetamines, often prescribed to promote weight loss, to be more highly addictive than doctors and scientists originally thought. In 1975, this new evidence compelled experts to reclassify amphetamines and move them from Schedule III to Schedule II.

The law also permits drugs to be declassified. In 1984, the pain reliever ibuprofen, found in such over-the-counter medications as Advil and Nuprin, was removed from the schedule entirely. By monitoring drug use, as well as keeping abreast of new drugs that were coming on the market, the various drug enforcement agencies hoped not only to halt the flow of illegal drugs but, at the same time, to compile more complete information about the potential side effects of various medicines.

In addition to the scheduling system that classified drugs, the Controlled Substances Act outlined the penalties for the illegal manufacture and sale of drugs. Punishments ranged from fines of between $10,000 and $250,000 to lengthy jail sentences. They were assessed according to

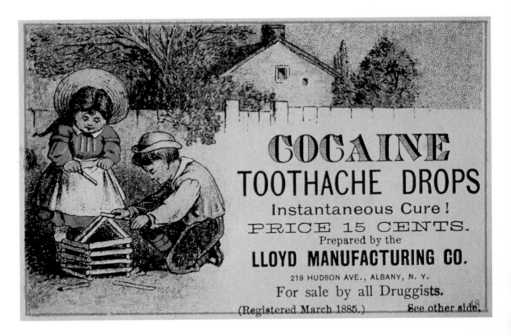

COCAINE
TOOTHACHE DROPS
Instantaneous Cure!
PRICE 15 CENTS.
Prepared by the
LLOYD MANUFACTURING CO.
219 HUDSON AVE., ALBANY, N. Y.
For sale by all Druggists.
(Registered March 1885.) See other side.

whether a person was convicted of a first offense or had broken the law more than once.

With the passage of the Controlled Substances Act, the United States government had made clear the gravity of the war on drugs. Congress continued to vote for additional funds and to authorize the creation of additional drug enforcement agencies. In 1972, three more organizations were formed:

1. the Office of National Narcotics Intelligence, and
2. the Office of Drug Abuse Law Enforcement, both of which were branches of the Department of Justice, and
3. the Narcotics Advance Research Management Team, which was under the direction of the executive branch.

The U.S. Customs Service, another division of the Treasury Department, also had its own antidrug group, called the Special Drug Investigations Unit, which dealt

During the early 1900s, advertisements, such as this one for a toothache remedy made with cocaine, offered little warning of the damage some drugs were capable of causing. Although many drugs were outlawed, it wasn't until 1970 that a classification system helped to clearly define the dangers some drugs posed.

In 1973, President Richard Nixon reorganized a number of separate agencies into one combined effort and created the Drug Enforcement Administration. The agency's mission is putting an end to the illegal flow of drugs into the United States.

exclusively with drug smuggling. Even the Federal Bureau of Investigation (FBI), found itself investigating drug-related cases in which drug trafficking was connected to organized crime.

With all of these groups gathering information and conducting investigations, it was only a matter of time before their activities became a muddle of official confusion. Although the agencies were supposed to work together, there was ongoing resistance to interagency cooperation, combined with the struggle not to duplicate each other's work. Before long, it became completely apparent to President Richard M. Nixon that something needed to be done to make the war on drugs more efficient.

As a consequence, in July 1973, President Nixon approved a plan to organize yet another new agency to oversee all antidrug efforts. This new agency was to be known as the Drug Enforcement Administration, also called the

Drug Enforcement Agency, or DEA. It would serve as the primary vehicle for the enforcement of drug laws. A division of the Justice Department, the DEA was authorized to coordinate the activities of the five other drug enforcement agencies. The director of the DEA was to report directly to the attorney general of the United States.

The stated mission of the DEA was "to interdict [stop] the highest levels of the illicit [illegal] drug traffic" in the United States and to prevent illegal drugs from entering the country, even if it meant interfering in the affairs of foreign governments. This objective was clearly stated. Yet the agents of the DEA quickly learned that they had their work cut out for them.

In the past, the use of habit-forming drugs was not unusual in the medical field. It would have been common for a surgeon's chest, such as this one from the late 1800s, to contain the highly addictive drugs opium, morphine, and heroin.

CHAPTER 2

An Ongoing War

DRUGS HAVE ALWAYS BEEN present in society. Not until the 20th century, however, did certain types of drugs become classified as "illegal." Until then, drug use was controlled by means of social pressure rather than criminal law. In fact, before 1850, many drugs now categorized as illegal, such as marijuana, cocaine, and opium, were widely used throughout Asia, Europe, Africa, and the Americas. At that time, no political or legal authority even raised the possibility of outlawing or limiting these substances.

There are, though, important differences between the "drug culture" of the past and the "drug culture" of the present. For one thing, people tended to use a single type of drug. A society flooded with a vast array of different drugs was unknown. Before the 15th century, for instance, Europeans drank beer and wine. In China, people smoked opium. Native Americans used peyote, often as part of their religious ceremonies. Beginning with the journeys of Christopher Columbus to

A British ship fires at a row of war junks during the Great Opium Wars of the mid-1800s. During this time period, doing business in drugs was considered an acceptable means of making money, and countries went to war to protect those rights.

the New World, new drugs found their way into Europe. Opium from the Far East and tobacco from America were among the most popular and the most profitable.

But even the influx of opium and tobacco brought little pressure on governments to regulate their sale and use. Plus, European merchants who trafficked in narcotics viewed this commerce as a legitimate business enterprise, akin to the selling of silks, spices, or any other commodity. Opium, in particular, brought huge profits, and traders eagerly took the business opportunity. Although awareness was growing that opium was addictive, many reasoned that only persons of weak moral character would fall prey to it. Little did merchants think that by importing and marketing opium and other drugs they were contributing to a new and dangerous social problem.

The Chinese had come to regard the matter differently. Knowing the harmful effects of opium addiction, the Chinese emperor banned its use among his subjects in 1729. In 1833, treaties between China and the United States prohibited American citizens from taking part in the Far East drug trade. The British, on the contrary, kept expanding their commerce in drugs. British merchants dominated the opium markets of Persia, Turkey, Egypt, and India. The British desire to control the opium trade in China led to war. Although the Chinese themselves were forbidden to use opium, the Manchu dynasty that ruled China had granted a monopoly (exclusive market) to certain Chinese merchants to export it. Officials of the British East India Company, however, claimed the right to enter into the Chinese opium trade. When the Chinese destroyed a supply of opium belonging to the British East India Company, the British government declared war. In the Great Opium Wars, fought from 1839 to 1842 and from 1856 to 1858, British forces crushed Chinese resistance and forced open the opium markets of the Far East to British merchants. Their triumph, though, came at a moment when many Europeans were rethinking their attitudes toward drug use.

By the early 19th century, opium was readily available throughout the Western world. Often people consumed opium in the form of pills or mixed it with alcohol. This compound was known as *laudanum*. In Great Britain, chemists (pharmacists) advertised opium as an over-the-counter remedy for a variety of ills. Doctors commonly prescribed the drug for their patients. One physician even described opium as "a commodity like so much tea."

In addition, by this time scientists had learned how to extract morphine from opium. Morphine is a strong **sedative** and **anaesthetic.** The practice of medicine during the 19th century was still primitive in many respects. Doctors were grateful to have at last come across a drug that could ease the suffering of their patients. Yet, as doctors began prescribing heavy doses of both opium and morphine, often to ease pain after surgery, they noticed that many of their patients developed new health problems. Most persons who took opium and morphine for an extended period of time became addicts. Ironically, by the late 1890s, in order to counteract the addictive effects of morphine, scientists developed another drug manufactured from opium: heroin. Many doctors mistakenly believed that by giving patients heroin instead of morphine they were substituting a nonaddictive drug for a habit-forming one. They could not have been more wrong.

But it was not simply opium and its offspring that were causing problems, for cocaine had also come into widespread use. Derived from the leaves of the coca plant, native to South America, cocaine was first made by German scientists in 1862. By the 1880s, doctors in the United States were using cocaine to help with opium addiction and to combat alcoholism. Sigmund Freud, the father of psychoanalysis, used cocaine in his early experiments but stopped prescribing it when he discovered its highly addictive nature. Like opium, cocaine was also frequently an ingredient in nonprescription drugs. It was even used in popular soft drinks such as Coca-Cola. Cocaine even gained literary fame when Sir Arthur Conan Doyle made it the drug of choice for his famous fictional detective Sherlock Holmes. Yet, Doyle also had Holmes's friend and colleague Dr. Watson warn him about the terrible effects of the drug. Watson repeatedly cautions Holmes against "a pathological and morbid process" of cocaine addiction.

In the United States, the first real drug epidemic flourished between 1850 and 1914. In the 1850s, thousands of Chinese immigrants came to the United States. Many arrived in California, where they found work mining gold or building railroads. The Chinese brought with them a strong work ethic and a powerful desire to make a better life for themselves. They also brought something less wholesome: the practice of smoking opium. By the 1870s, smoking opium, once thought to be the exclusive bane of the Chinese, had spread to what was called the "sporting classes," which included gamblers, thieves, prostitutes, musicians, and actors.

Sigmund Freud once used cocaine for his experiments until he discovered its addictive qualities. In the 19th century drugs were often used by both scientists and doctors with little knowledge of or regard for the harm they were causing.

Gradually, opium use became fashionable and spread to segments of the American middle and upper classes. Opium dens, in which addicts could buy and smoke opium, began appearing in a number of cities throughout the United States. The growing availability of opium spurred a general movement to prohibit drug use. Saloons that served alcohol had been the target of an earlier crusade against vice. By the late 19th century, though, advocates of **prohibition** attacked the sale and use of other drugs such as opiates and cocaine and even tobacco. But government regulation of drugs did not begin until the last years of the 19th century. Then several cities and states passed laws that restricted the drug trade. In many cases, these laws were as much attempts to overpower a particular ethnic or racial minority, such as Asians or African Americans, as they were to outlaw the sale and use of drugs. A law enacted by the city council of San Francisco, California, in 1875, for example, banned the opium dens that were located in Chinatown, a measure clearly aimed at controlling the Chinese population.

By the early 1900s, the medical profession and the general public, alarmed by what now seemed to many a grave social problem, lobbied for state controls to restrict the sale and use of narcotics. Not until 1914, though, with the passage of the Harrison Act, did the federal government enact a national antidrug code. Even the Harrison Act was more of a tax measure than a prohibition on drug use. According to the act, a federal tax of one cent was to be collected on each ounce of opium and coca products sold. The law also required anyone who shipped, handled, prescribed, or sold such products to register with the government and keep detailed records of every transaction. Only members of the medical profession could legally obtain a registration. Furthermore, doctors caught prescribing drugs for addicts were subject to arrest, **prosecution,** and imprisonment.

The Internal Revenue Service (IRS), a division of the Treasury Department, assigned 162 agents and collectors to its Miscellaneous Division to administer the Harrison Act. These early efforts were the first national drug enforcement measures adopted in the United States and provided the model for the DEA.

Addicts were prevented from legally getting drugs, so many then turned to other ways to acquire them. By the 1920s, drug smuggling, usually controlled by organized criminal gangs, was the primary source for illegal drugs.

MENS CELLROOM

The sale of narcotics fell into the hands of gangsters and criminal organizations following its outlawing in the early 1900s. Throughout our country's history there have always been individuals willing to break the law in order to provide or consume illegal narcotics.

Treasury agents were not slow to recognize the direct connection between drug dealing and organized crime. If the federal government not only hoped to control drug use but to crack down on organized crime, it would have to increase the resources allocated to the effort.

Unfortunately, during the 1920s, agents for the Treasury Department had their hands full trying to implement the 18th Amendment. Passed in 1919, the Volstead Act, which provided for the enforcement of the 18th Amendment, banned the manufacture, transport, and sale of alcoholic beverages in the United States. This was called the Prohibition era. The Treasury Department, already charged with enforcing the Harrison Act, now also had to execute the Volstead Act. The assets and manpower of the department were spread too thinly to be effective.

As a result, the effort to enforce Prohibition and, at the same time, to eliminate illegal drugs, was doomed to failure from the start. "Rumrunners" and drug smugglers were often the same people. But the powerful criminal groups that controlled the illegal trade in drugs and alcohol often prevented agents from making arrests or, if they did make arrests, from getting convictions. Although faced with a daunting, nearly impossible, task, the Treasury Department did not give up without a fight. To combat the spread of illegal drugs, the department created the Bureau of Prohibition. With the aid of state and local law enforcement agencies, Treasury investigators worked tirelessly to stop the flow of alcohol and drugs. Predictably, they enjoyed only mixed results.

Recognizing the futility of outlawing alcohol, Congress repealed the 18th Amendment in 1933 and brought Prohibition to an end. In the meantime, though, legislators had also created another new agency whose sole purpose was to enforce drug laws. The Bureau of Narcotics, founded in 1930, had broad powers and responsibilities to enforce new laws such as the Marijuana Tax Act of 1937. This legislation made both marijuana and hashish illegal substances. In the mid-1950s, Congress enacted even tighter laws targeting both drug dealers and drug users. This new series of laws carried **mandatory** jail sentences for those convicted of a violation. In some cases, dealers found guilty of selling heroin to minors faced the death penalty.

By the mid-1960s, federal officials could state with confidence that these statutes had produced results. Estimates suggested that at one time there had been nearly a million drug addicts in the United States. By 1965, figures showed a decline to about 600,000. Although drug use seemed to be in decline, the Bureau of Narcotics still could not afford to relax. Despite tighter laws, drugs were still big business and, worse, remained under the control of aggressive criminal organizations. That made the drug problem more difficult than ever to solve.

The statistics did not reveal that the government's nightmare was just beginning. The casual drug use promoted by members of the **counterculture** during the 1960s began to increase in the early 1970s. When many of the 76

million baby boomers began not only to experiment with drugs, but to grow, manufacture, and sell them, the drug culture expanded many times over. Drug use peaked in 1979 when a published report indicated that one in every 10 Americans used drugs on a regular basis. Joining marijuana as a preferred drug was cocaine, often called the "champagne of drugs" because of its cost. By the middle of the 1980s, more than six million Americans routinely used illegal drugs. Drug abuse in the United States was widespread.

In the 1980s, too, reports surfaced about a destructive new drug that was very addictive and unpredictable in its effects. Even worse, it was easy and cheap to manufacture and sell. The drug was crack cocaine. Its appearance marked a heightening of the drug crisis in the United States. For law enforcement agencies, the war on drugs had taken an even deadlier turn.

During the counterculture movement of the 1960s, many people accepted the casual use of drugs such as marijuana and LSD. As drugs became more readily available and use became widespread, it became apparent that the problems caused by drug use in the United States were growing.

CHAPTER **3**

The Inner DEA

HEIDI HERRERA WAS VISIBLY nervous as she sat alone in the bare interview room of the DEA offices in San Diego. A few minutes later, DEA agents led two Colombians, members of a large Colombian drug **cartel,** into the room. Upon seeing Heidi, one of the men looked relieved. Known as the daughter of a retired Mexican drug lord, Herrera had arranged a meeting that was to have taken place later that day between these men and her father. She had a reputation for "laundering" drug money, the process whereby drug dealers convert illegal profits into legitimate money that authorities cannot trace to a crime. She was also well known for brokering high-stakes drug deals.

The Colombians never made the meeting that Herrera had set. Moments after they left her luxurious office, they were arrested by agents for the DEA. They were now awaiting questioning about their connection with Herrera and the cartel.

When the Colombians entered the room, Heidi whispered to one of the agents, "Que les digo?" ("What should I tell them?") Without waiting for an answer, she turned to the two men and said calmly: "My name's Heidi Landgraf. I'm an agent with the DEA." They stared at her in stunned silence and disbelief. After two years and countless man-hours, "Operation Green Ice" was over.

Before the end of the workday, police in the United States, along with law enforcement officials in six other countries, had arrested 140 suspected criminals and seized more than $50 million. More important, the operation had dealt a severe blow to members of the Colombian drug cartels. Although more than 100 DEA agents had participated in Operation Green Ice, it was the hard work and courage of Heidi Landgraf that ultimately made the enterprise such a resounding success.

Operating undercover as Heidi Herrera, Landgraf made multimillion dollar deals by helping to launder money for the various drug cartels. Working through a team of informants and with the help of video cameras in her "office," Herrera met a number of individuals involved in the international drug trade. As one agent later described it, she "went up against criminals who would cut your heart out in a second."

Heidi Landgraf's activities represent just one aspect of a DEA agent's job. Helping her were hundreds of other individuals whose task it is to make sure the agency is always ready to take on drug dealers. Carrying out that mission is never easy, and it requires an elaborate and many-sided effort. The operation of the DEA, then, is as complex as some of its undercover operations.

The DEA is headed by an administrator who is nominated by the president of the United States and whose appointment must be approved by Congress. Since its creation there have been six administrators who have managed

the DEA. These people have come from a variety of backgrounds. They include a superintendent of the New York State Police, a former U.S. district judge from California, and an ex-FBI agent who also served as a front office executive for the New York Yankees! The seventh, and most recent, appointee is Donnie Marshall, a native of Texas. Prior to his appointment as administrator, he served as deputy administrator of the DEA. Marshall is the first DEA administrator to be promoted to the post from within the agency itself.

In order to carry out its duties as successfully as possible, the DEA has broken down its primary goal, winning the war on drugs, into several areas of activity. First, the agency investigates all major violations of state and

Donnie Marshall, seen here on the right, speaks with the director of drug control policy, Barry McCaffrey, during a hearing on the legalization of marijuana. Marshall is the first administrator of the DEA to have been appointed from within the organization.

An armed DEA agent stands guard next to over $25 million worth of cocaine seized in Baltimore, Maryland. Agents are trained in the use of a number of firearms as well as being skilled in hand-to-hand combat.

national drug laws. Second, the DEA is charged with making sure all federal drug laws are enforced, including those that regulate the *legal* manufacture, distribution, and sale of controlled substances. Third, the DEA gathers and manages all information used in drug enforcement. Fourth, the DEA works with other federal law enforcement agencies such as the FBI, with local and state officials, and with such international bureaus as Interpol (the International Police) and the United Nations Commission on Narcotics. Together they coordinate the worldwide assault on illegal drugs. Fifth, the DEA designs and implements training and research programs to foster drug education.

To accomplish these diverse activities, the DEA employs 9,035 persons. Of this number, 4,515 are the special agents who occupy the front lines of the war on drugs. There are 522 diversion investigators busy scrutinizing cases of legally manufactured drugs that have been "diverted" through

illegal sales. Some 681 intelligence specialists have the time-consuming task of analyzing the thousands of pieces of information and evidence that field agents have compiled. The 256 chemists who work at the DEA study and evaluate the effects of drugs on the body and the brain. A staff of 1,808 technical and clerical workers and 1,253 lawyers and administrators oversee daily operations.

The national headquarters of the DEA is in Arlington, Virginia, but the agency has 20 divisional offices throughout the United States in Atlanta, Boston, Chicago, Dallas, Denver, Detroit, El Paso, Houston, Los Angeles, Miami, Newark, New Orleans, New York, Philadelphia, Phoenix, San Diego, San Francisco, Seattle, St. Louis, and Washington, D.C. In addition, the DEA has a Caribbean Divisional

An anti-narcotics team from the Colombian military patrol a river in the depths of the Colombian jungle. The DEA works closely with the international community to fight the traffic of drugs into the United States and maintains divisional offices all across the globe.

Office, which monitors drug activities in Puerto Rico, Haiti, the Dominican Republic, Jamaica, and Barbados.

To survey international drug activity, the DEA also has 78 divisional offices established in 56 countries, including Europe, the Mideast, the Far East, Africa, and Central and South America. In the year 2000, two new offices opened in Hanoi, Vietnam, and Tashkent, Uzbekistan. The DEA has more than one office in areas where there is a great deal of drug trafficking, such as in Thailand, Mexico, Colombia, and Bolivia.

The DEA supports five regional forensic laboratories that evaluate valuable evidence. These facilities are found in Chicago, Miami, San Diego, San Francisco, and Washington, D.C. A sixth lab, known as the Special Testing and Research Laboratory, located in McLean, Virginia, provides forensic help to all DEA foreign offices and on occasion to the regional labs as well. There are also two satellite labs—one in Kansas City, Missouri, and another in San Juan, Puerto Rico.

Within the DEA itself there are a number of specialized departments called "offices" that are responsible for specific DEA operations. The Office of Chief Counsel handles all legal affairs, advises local, state, and federal prosecutors on the progress of drug cases, and represents the agency or individual agents if they happened to be named in a lawsuit or accused of a crime.

The Office of Congressional and Public Affairs directs all communications between the DEA, federal lawmakers, and the public. Among other things, this office publishes special reports, statistics, public relations articles, and other information that notifies the public about the actions and accomplishments of the DEA.

The Board of Professional Standards makes sure that agents and other employees of the DEA maintain appropriate conduct on and off the job. To enforce DEA rules, the Office of Professional Responsibility, which is part of the larger Planning and Inspection Division, investigates charges of misconduct. In 1995, for instance, the Office of Professional Responsibility launched a probe of DEA agents accused of using "unprofessional language" in training sessions with local law enforcement. The office has also looked into charges of racial discrimination brought by agents against the DEA. Each of these divisions is small and reports directly to the administrator.

The majority of the employees at the DEA work in one of three larger divisions: the Planning and Inspection Division, the Operational Support Division, or the Operations Division. Within each of these offices are several smaller units, each performing specific tasks. The Planning and Inspection Division takes care of the long-term management of DEA programs and activities as well as the evaluation of the agency's performance. More routine matters such as hiring, budgeting, and purchasing are the responsibility of the Operational Support Division. This department also houses the Office of Science and Technology, which is in charge of the day-to-day operation of the DEA's forensic laboratories.

The Operations Division keeps field offices running smoothly and monitors and protects agents and other operatives. In cooperation with law enforcement agencies around the world, the Operations Division also uses two measures designed to eliminate illegal drugs at their source. The first of these is crop eradication, in which fields of coca, marijuana, and poppy plants (used to make opium and heroin), are destroyed by burning or chemical spraying. The second is crop substitution, a program that encourages farmers to grow legal crops.

Two other important offices are housed in the Operations Division: the Office of Intelligence (OI) and the

Following a combined effort by the DEA and the Mexican army, nine tons of cocaine and three tons of marijuana are destroyed by fire. Crop eradication and the burning of seized drugs are techniques often employed by the DEA.

Office of Diversion Control (ODC). Gathering, organizing, and evaluating information about drug-related activities is the responsibility of the Office of Intelligence. This material is then used in two ways. First, the OI creates reports on known drug kingpins and current drug enterprises in the United States and throughout the world. Second, the OI makes long-term predictions about the production, distribution, and sale of illegal drugs and long-range strategies for how best to stop these endeavors.

The Office of Diversion Control makes sure that the Controlled Substances Act is upheld. This branch of the DEA supervises more than 750,000 doctors, pharmacists, and other hospital workers who handle or prescribe drugs in the United States. They also carefully inspect drug manufacturers and distributors. Investigators for the ODC make certain that these companies maintain adequate security to prevent theft. They also look into all cases of "diversion" in which prescription drugs have somehow been obtained for illegal sale and use. The ODC also determines whether drugmakers and distributors are engaged only in legal activities or are instead functioning as fronts for criminal organizations. Like the other divisions of the DEA, the ODC also works closely with local and state law enforcement agencies in conducting these investigations.

One of the most important offices in the DEA is the Office of Training. Until 1987, DEA training programs were carried out at the Federal Law Enforcement Training Center in Glynco, Georgia. Beginning in 1988, however, DEA training was consolidated with FBI training and is now conducted in 15-week sessions at the Quantico, Virginia, federal training center. To become a DEA agent a candidate must be between 21 and 35 years of age, pass a series of physical examinations, and have a valid driver's license. Prospective agents must also have three years of general work experience or have spent at least two years in military service or law enforcement. For this reason, many of those who become special agents for the DEA transfer from other federal agencies, such as the FBI or the Bureau of Alcohol, Tobacco, and Firearms (ATF). Alternately, a candidate may have a bachelor's degree from an accredited college or university or certification as a public accountant.

A candidate who meets the physical, educational, and other qualifications faces two additional tests. One is an interview with a panel of DEA officials to evaluate his or her intellectual capacity and mental stability. The second is an intensive look into the candidate's background. Drug Enforcement Administration reviewers question family members, friends, former and current employers, teachers, and anyone else in a position to know precise and intimate details of the candidate's life. They also examine school

DEA agents train in Quantico, Virginia, using a replica of a small town. Applicants are required to meet a long list of requirements in order to be considered for employment within the DEA.

and employment records and, if relevant, military and police records. A minor criminal offense, even a traffic violation, is enough to disqualify an applicant. Any illegal drug use, of course, brings automatic rejection.

DEA trainees must learn how to use a variety of weapons and master the techniques of hand-to-hand combat. They must also thoroughly understand drug laws, such as the Controlled Substances Act, and know the principles of drug and forensic chemistry. They have to comprehend the art of conducting **surveillance,** the legal guidelines for search and seizure, the procedure and method for **interrogating** suspects, and the ways to track drug profits. Drug dealers hide money in a maze of secret bank accounts, overseas investments, laundering operations, and computerized transactions.

Becoming a DEA agent is not easy, and the life of an agent is far from exciting most of the time. It is not always even very safe. Yet, for the men and women who qualify, survive the training, and take their place at the DEA, the reward comes from knowing that they are doing their part to end the sale and use of illegal drugs.

The DEA uses resources such as this forensic lab to help prosecute criminals who profit from the creation and sale of illegal drugs. The DEA manages eight forensic laboratories across the country.

CHAPTER **4**

Special Programs and Task Forces

IN ADDITION TO THE different divisions and offices that compose the DEA, there are a number of programs to help manage all the information gathered by agents in their ongoing investigations. All of these systems, which are run by the most up-to-date computer technology, are operated by the Office of Intelligence or the Office of Science and Technology.

Some of these systems include:

★ DATS, or the DEA Automated Teleprocessing System. This serves as an international communications system for the agency. DATS enables agents from anywhere in the world to access DEA intelligence files over the telephone.

★ DEA Communications, a nationwide radio and teletype system, directly links DEA offices with the Department of State and the Department of Defense.

★ The Narcotics and Dangerous Drugs Information System, or NADDIS, is a database that contains more than two million records on individuals and businesses that may be involved or employed in illegal drug activity. This system is also connected to the three databases of the FBI: the National Crime Center, the Wanted Persons File, and the Stolen Gun File.

★ STRIDE, or the System to Retrieve Information from Drug Evidence, contains information that has been gathered by the administration's forensic laboratories. This is especially useful in studying new or existing trends in drug trafficking and use and in estimating the strength and availability of a particular drug.

★ The Drug Theft Reporting System, or DTRS, provides information about the theft or loss of any controlled substance. There are also separate databases for information related to the Controlled Substances Act as well as information about the manufacture, distribution, and sale of controlled substances by those registered to handle them.

★ Just because a drug offender has been arrested does not mean that the DEA stops investigating. With the OBTS, or Offender Based Transaction System, the agency continues to follow a criminal's movement through the justice system.

The DEA also has databases that keep track of its current activities, the status of its field agents and informants, its financial records, and various expenses and budget reports. In addition, the DEA works closely with the National Institute on Drug Abuse to collect information from hospital emergency rooms, drug crisis centers, and coroners' offices to determine which drugs are being most frequently bought, sold, and abused.

A law enforcement officer holds up rounds of body-armor piercing ammunition seized during a drug raid in Los Angeles, California. As more advanced weaponry becomes available to criminals, the job of the DEA becomes increasingly dangerous.

There are also a number of cooperative programs in which the DEA participates to meet the specific needs of state and local drug enforcement authorities. Among the most important of these is the Marijuana Eradication Program. Today, marijuana is the most widely used and readily available illegal drug in the United States. The MEP is just one way in which the DEA combats the expansion of marijuana growing in the United States.

Another is the Domestic Cannabis Eradication and Suppression Program (DCE/SP), which exclusively targets marijuana.

Begun in 1979 in California and Hawaii, the DCE/SP has since expanded to include all 50 states, while spending $13.5 million annually to support 87 state and local agencies. Pooling resources and sharing knowledge has allowed the DEA and its partners to locate and destroy marijuana crops grown both indoors and outdoors. New technology, such as thermal imaging, has helped to pinpoint the location of indoor marijuana crops by registering the heat from lamps used in indoor growing.

As of early 2000, the program had destroyed 2.3 million marijuana plants grown indoors, 232,839 plants grown outdoors, and an additional 89,303 pounds of processed bulk marijuana. In addition, the DCE/SP has led to the seizure of more than 8,700 weapons and almost $30 million in assets. It has also enabled federal, state, and local drug enforcement officers to make 13,603 arrests.

Another important DEA program is Financial Investigations. Agents trained as accountants and financial lawyers work closely with investigators from the IRS and the U.S. Customs Service to examine the financial records of individuals and companies suspected of having taken part in illegal drug transactions. When an arrest is made, the DEA uses asset **forfeiture** (giving up) as a means of recovering evidence and money from drug-related crimes. In the United States, federal law states that profits gained from illegal activities, as well as all property used in, or acquired as the result of, such crimes (such as houses, automobiles, boats, art objects, and the like) are subject to forfeiture.

The money and property that the DEA appropriates are channeled into a number of programs. Some assets are put into the Asset Forfeiture Fund, which aids the victims of crime. In one case, two houses seized from a drug dealer in Philadelphia were given to United Neighbors Against Drugs. The homes have since been turned into a community center, which now houses a job-skills training program, a drug prevention office, and a "safe house" for neighborhood children.

Another instance of federal, state, and local cooperation is the State and Local Task Force. This effort actually began in 1970, three years before the formation of the Drug Enforcement Administration. It has since worked to establish its presence at all levels of drug enforcement. Realizing that the agency could never win the war on drugs alone, DEA officials encouraged cooperation with local and state authorities. Often the DEA assists localities in which law enforcement is sparse. By utilizing the information and technology available from DEA sources, state and local police have mounted more successful investigations. By 1999, the DEA State and Local Task Force consisted of 188 affiliates staffed by more than 1,000 DEA agents and 1,800 state and local police officers.

In 1982, the Organized Crime and Drug Enforcement Task Force (OCDETF) was developed. This further coordinates the federal, state, and local assault on organized crime and drug trafficking. Today, the OCDETF employs more 1,000 persons, including 775 special agents, and has been very successful in combining its efforts with those of local and state law enforcement agencies. From the beginning, the desired outcome of this initiative has been the arrest and conviction of key underworld bosses and the disabling of their criminal and drug empires.

The involvement of organized crime in drug trafficking dates from the 1920s. But since World War II, organized crime, particularly the Mafia, has been responsible for the largest percentage of illegal drugs coming into the United States. By the 1970s, though, control of the

Salvatore "Sammy the Bull" Gravano, a former member of the Gotti crime syndicate, stands trial for his involvement in the sale of the designer drug Ecstasy. Organized crime still plays a large role in the importing of illegal substances.

drug trade was slipping from the grasp of older criminal organizations and into the hands of black and Hispanic urban gangs. The influx of South American drug cartels, clans from China and Southeast Asia, and mobsters from Jamaica and Russia have complicated matters. Today several groups are competing to control the networks of supply and distribution as well as the clients and the profits of the drug trade. This diversity makes it much harder for the DEA to concentrate its efforts.

To fight these many criminal elements, therefore, the OCDETF has started a number of new programs in recent years. One **initiative,** known as "Weed and Seed," endeavors to clean up neighborhoods, making them less attractive to drug dealers and other criminals. The High Intensity Drug

Trafficking Areas (HIDTA) project targets zones known for a high volume of drug trafficking, such as the Gulf Coast, New York City, and South Florida, from where drugs are shipped to other parts of the country. Since its inception in 1988, this program has grown from five target areas to more than 31 locations throughout the country, including five trafficking areas along the southwestern border of the United States. All are designed to intercept illegal drugs at their source of entry.

Two intelligence divisions within the DEA also stress interagency and multilevel cooperation. The El Paso Intelligence Center (EPIC), located in El Paso, Texas, was established in 1974 to study and set policy for dealing with drug and border problems. Agents from the DEA, the Immigration and Naturalization Service (INS), and the U.S. Customs Service explore the connections between drug trafficking, immigration violations, weapons and explosives **smuggling,** and vehicle theft.

Initially, the EPIC focused solely on criminal activities in the southwestern United States. With the aid of more sophisticated surveillance and tracking technology, however, the EPIC has taken on a more national focus. The office now has partnerships in all 50 states, Puerto Rico, the Virgin Islands, and Guam. In addition, in 1998, the EPIC entered into an information-sharing partnership with the premier law enforcement agency in Canada, the Royal Canadian Mounted Police.

The second, and one of the latest, cooperative efforts came in 1992 with the establishment of the National Drug Pointer Index (NDPIX), through which the DEA, in conjunction with other law enforcement agencies, coordinates drug investigations. With the introduction of this new program, the duplication of investigations, which wastes valuable time, money, and man power, has been reduced. As of April 1999, the NDPIX had entered more than

The premier law enforcement agency in Canada, the Royal Canadian Mounted Police, have often worked in cooperation with the DEA to ensure that drug trafficking does not take place along the United States/Canada border.

40,000 drug investigation targets into its database. As more law enforcement agencies come to participate in these new initiatives, investigations will become even more effective in combating the illegal drug trade.

The DEA also works at educating Americans, especially the young, about the perils of drug abuse. In a series of publications with titles like *Get It Straight*, the DEA has covered such topics as drug prevention in schools and the establishment of the drug-free workplace. The agency also makes available to the general public other publications, such as the transcripts of expert testimony before Congress about drug use, agency intelligence and technical reports, drug identification sheets, and press releases detailing the continuing efforts and achievements of the DEA. By instructing the American people about the dangers of drug addiction, the DEA, of course, hopes to stop the problem before it starts. Prevention is the best and surest way of winning the war on drugs.

Thomas A. Constantine was criticized for his leadership of the Drug Enforcement Administration and for conflicts which arose with the FBI during his tenure. Steps have recently been taken to provide more cooperation between the DEA and other law enforcement agencies.

CHAPTER 5

The Future of the DEA

THE DEA CELEBRATED ITS 25th anniversary in 1998. To mark the occasion, the agency issued a special press release in which then administrator Thomas A. Constantine pledged that the DEA would continue to dedicate itself to "serving and protecting the American people by providing the best federal drug law enforcement in communities around the nation."

Constantine's heroic declaration, however, could not conceal the growing problems within the agency. For nearly a decade, tension had mounted between the DEA and other federal rivals, notably the FBI. Representatives of the Justice Department were often frustrated in their attempts to settle disputes about the specific role and responsibilities of each agency. A principal source of strain was the general unwillingness to share information about ongoing investigations.

A Justice Department internal memo that accidentally found its way into newspapers stated that "the overall relationship [between the DEA and the FBI] is unproductively competitive and seems to be worsening." The memo went on to state that if the issues preventing greater cooperation between the two agencies could not be resolved, then both might lose their independent status and end by being merged into a single bureau. Although a spokesman for the Drug Enforcement Administration refused to comment on the memo, one FBI official tried to minimize its importance by stating that "When two organizations with the same **jurisdiction** are aggressive, there are going to be some bumps and grinds."

Aside from the trouble with outside agencies, the internal workings of the DEA were tense as well. Under Constantine's leadership, the agency was at war with itself, afflicted by suspicion, bitterness, and worse, rebelliousness, on the part of many agents toward their chief. In describing the situation, one former DEA employee stated that Constantine "has no respect for the agency or the agents, and so they have no respect for him. I don't know of a single man in upper management who's happy with what this guy's doing."

Many agents were displeased with Constantine's "no-nonsense, paramilitary management style" in an agency known for taking bold but necessary risks. Others accused the administrator of trying to cripple the DEA and thereby unwittingly opening the way for the FBI to seize the initiative in the war on drugs. Unfortunately, the DEA and the FBI spent almost as much time during the 1990s bickering with each other and among themselves as they did in subduing criminals.

Part of the problem the DEA faced during the decade was confusion about where best to concentrate its efforts. Under both Constantine and his predecessor Robert Bonner, who served as agency head from 1990 until 1993, the

DEA's budget was cut while the rate of drug offenses soared. Although the DEA's yearly operating budget now exceeds $1 billion, (the figure for 1999 was $1.41 billion), the agency has, at times, found itself overwhelmed by the escalating war on drugs. Some criticized the agency for not paying enough attention to the international drug cartels. Others said efforts should be focused on local-level drug problems. As a result, the agency often found itself floundering, with the directors unsure of what to do next.

Despite these problems, though, and with a new administrator at the helm, the DEA has resolved to keep pace with drug crime at the dawn of the new millennium. By targeting illegal drug activity at all levels, the DEA has won some significant victories in the ongoing war on drugs. The most important accomplishments include:

★ The Southwest Border Initiative, established in 1994, which is another cooperative effort between the DEA and local authorities to stop Mexican drug

A customs agent stops a car traveling across the border between Mexico and the United States. Recent initiatives between the DEA and southwestern law enforcement bodies have stepped up attempts to stop the trafficking of drugs along the United States/Mexico border.

trafficking along the southwestern border of the United States. Working with the FBI and Customs, the SWBI targets the communications systems of Mexican drug lords in order to chart the movement of illegal drugs. Three particular operations, Operation Zorro II, Operation Reciprocity (mutual action), and Operation Limelight, ended with the arrest of 156 persons, the seizure of 22,000 kilos of various drugs including cocaine and heroin, and the recovery of $35 million in assets. The SWBI has also reduced the level of bribery and corruption among law enforcement officers and border guards and limited the transport of illegal aliens to the United States.

★ In 1995, the DEA set up the Woodward Academy, a residential school in Detroit, Michigan, for at-risk children. Two hundred boys and girls from the 5th to 9th grades attend the school year-round. The DEA hopes that Woodward Academy will provide a much needed alternative to the drug-infested and crime-ridden inner-city schools that most of these students would have to otherwise attend. If this is successful, the agency plans to open similar schools in other cities where there are high concentrations of drugs that place children at risk.

★ Also in 1995, the DEA created its MET program. MET, which stands for Mobile Enforcement Team, was designed to combat the drug problem in poorer neighborhoods and communities across the United States, where a police presence is often too little or completely lacking. Working again with local law enforcement agencies, the MET gathers and shares information, leading to more arrests and seizures of drugs, money, and assets. The MET also assists local, state, and federal prosecutors in getting convictions in drug-related cases. By October 1999, more than 400 MET units had been deployed. Since its inception, the program has led to more than 8,900 arrests and the confiscation of $20.4 million in cash and property. Drug seizures have included 1,516 pounds of cocaine, 468 pounds of methamphetamine, 67 pounds of heroin, and 2,756 pounds of marijuana.

★ Another undertaking has been the expansion of the DEA aviation program, now known as the Office of Aviation Operations, or OA. When it began in 1973, this division consisted of 24 aircraft and 41 special agents/pilots. Today, the OA has 95 planes and 117 special agents/pilots. They provide aviation support to domestic DEA offices as well as air-to-ground, air-to-water, and air-to-air electronic and photographic information-gathering.

★ In April 1999, the DEA opened its own museum. Located in the lobby of the DEA headquarters in Arlington, Virginia, this facility features an exhibit called "Illegal Drugs in America: A Modern History." The display illustrates the evolution of drug use and drug enforcement in the United States. The DEA museum is the only one in the country that deals specifically with what is widely acknowledged to be among the worst social problems in American history. The museum is yet another endeavor by the DEA to educate the public on the dangers of drugs.

During the last 15 years, the DEA has made a number of record-setting drug seizures, both nationally and internationally. On the national level these have included the recovery of 75,066 pounds of hashish and 388,113 pounds of marijuana in 1988, 47,554 pounds of cocaine in 1989, and 1,071 pounds of heroin in 1991. Internationally, the DEA impounded 4.3 million pounds of marijuana in Mexico

Although arresting the people responsible for drug trafficking is one of the DEA's main goals, the seizure of drugs, money, and weapons is also highly important. Not only does it stop drugs from entering the country, it also places added pressure on the gangs and cartels who transport narcotics.

in 1984, 2,816 pounds of heroin in Thailand in 1988, and 290,400 pounds of hashish from Pakistan in 1995.

As the business of drug trafficking has become more sophisticated, profitable, and violent, the DEA has had to be ever more imaginative and daring to outwit and catch criminals. Under the leadership of new administrator Donnie Marshall, the DEA has carried out several creative, if dangerous, operations, some employing unusual methods for undercover agents.

An airline pilot who mistakenly sipped a cup of coffee laced with heroin smuggled in the coffeemaker's filter led to "Operation Ramp Rat" and "Operation Sky Chef." These two-year undercover operations, in which special agents of the DEA posed as drug smugglers, culminated in the arrest of 58 airport employees at Miami International Airport in August 1999. Those arrested, many of whom were taken at their homes in a daring predawn raid, included 30 American Airlines ramp workers. Also arrested were a security guard, 13 employees of Sky Chef (an airline catering service), and three law enforcement officers, an immigration inspector, an agriculture inspector, and a deputy of the Broward County Sheriff's Department who worked part-time at the airport. Once in custody, these men and women were charged with smuggling cocaine, guns, and hand grenades aboard airplanes.

To crack a tough Colombian cocaine ring, the DEA resorted to an even more unusual ruse. This time the agents opened a fully licensed, but completely fictitious, stock-brokerage firm in Atlanta, Georgia. Members of the Colombian Cali cartel, one of the most powerful and notorious drug operations in the world, approached the agents posing as stockbrokers to launder money for them. For three years, the agents "agreed" to launder monies accrued through the buying and selling of cocaine. By the end of 1999, the sting operation ended with the arrest of 40 persons and the seizure of 3,500 kilos of cocaine and $10 million of laundered money.

In the fall of 1999 a DEA spokesman announced that "Operation Impunity" had concluded with the arrest of more than 90 members of a Mexican drug trafficking network and the seizure of more than $26 million in cash and assets, as well as the recovery of 13 tons of cocaine. Not long afterward, another undercover operation led to the arrest of more than 30 members of several Colombian drug cartels.

To show that the DEA means business, the agency, along with the U.S. Customs Service, recently seized nearly 3,000 pounds of cocaine and four ships at anchor in the Miami River. One ship alone yielded 1,000 pounds of cocaine! The confiscation of these drugs, which had a street value of more than $23 million, was part of an ongoing investigation begun in October 1997 into the activities of Haitian drug traffickers operating in South Florida. By the end of the affair, the DEA and the Customs Service had impounded more than 10,371 pounds of cocaine, 17 freighters, and $2.4 million in U.S. currency. In the process, the agency dealt a crippling blow to the Haitian and Colombian drug business.

Dramatic though these episodes may be, is any of this activity making a noticeable difference in the ongoing war on drugs? At first glance, the figures are somewhat encouraging. According to the results of a survey done by the Substance Abuse and Mental Health Services Administration and published in 1999, the number of Americans using drugs stands at an estimated 13.6 million persons. These figures constitute a significant decline compared with those compiled in 1979, when the number stood at 25.4 million. Nearly 1 in 10, or 9.9 percent, of youths ages 12–17 currently use drugs. This number also represents a significant drop from the 16.3 percent recorded in 1979, though it is not as low as the figure from a 1995 survey, when the number of youthful drug users stood at 5.3 percent.

Less heartening, during the late 1990s, there was a disturbing increase in the number of young adults aged 18–25 who used drugs. In 1999, 16.1 percent of Americans in this age group were regular drug users, as opposed to only 13.3 percent in 1994. Even more alarming is the growing popularity of heroin. In 1998, an estimated 130,000 Americans used heroin, compared to only 68,000 in 1993. That the number of heroin users in the United States nearly doubled in five years reflects, in part, the lower price and the easier availability of the drug. The average age of heroin users has also decreased from a high of 26.4 years of age in 1990 to 17.6 years in 1997. The use of "inhalants" such as glues and aerosols has also risen

Currently close to 10% of youths aged 12–17 use drugs on a regular basis. One of the main goals of the DEA in recent years has been to educate young people about the dangers of drug use.

at an alarming rate, up 95 percent since 1990. First-time inhalant users are also younger, with 65 percent between the ages of 12 and 17.

Even as the national crime rate decreased during the second half of the 1990s, the number of DEA arrests and seizures continued to climb. The use of the MET teams as well as other elite groups to target drug smuggling, especially among urban street gangs, has had a major impact on the increasing number of arrests. To the DEA, though, these figures only emphasize the need for continued vigilance and cooperation at all levels of law enforcement if the war on drugs is ever to be completely won.

Yet, victory, when and if it comes, will be at a high cost. Since the inception of federal laws restricting drugs and the establishment of an agency to enforce those laws, a total of 68 people, including special agents and other employees of the DEA, have lost their lives in the line of duty. In 1985, news of the grisly murder of DEA Special Agent Enrique Camarena, who was kidnapped and tortured to death by thugs in the service of a Mexican drug lord, saddened and outraged Americans. In memory of Camarena and others like him who have given their lives, many Americans began to don red ribbons. Today, many continue to wear a red ribbon during the last week of October to acknowledge their support for the men and women of the DEA who fight to create a drug-free America.

The danger of the battle over drugs continues to escalate. In February 2000, newspapers reported that the DEA had warned agents to take additional precautions after learning that a Mexican drug cartel had offered a $200,000 bounty for the killing of any federal officer. For DEA agents, especially those working the "pipeline" in the southeastern and southwestern United States, these safeguards meant not going out alone but always traveling in pairs. DEA officials tried to take the news in stride. One stated that "On average, once or twice a year, we hear a rumor of that nature. It's become a fact of life for us." No one, however, could ignore that the threat came just as a joint Mexican-FBI investigation into the discovery of a number of mass graves in Ciudad Juarez, Mexico, was getting underway. Some of the remains unearthed from these graves are thought to be those of drug agents or informants.

What is the biggest challenge facing the DEA in the future? According to Administrator Marshall, it is the current alliance of Mexican drug traffickers with the Colombian cartels. "It's an alliance that's more challenging than any drug trafficking group we've faced in the world," Marshall admits. There are, of course, also still the ongoing problems with drug trafficking in Haiti, the Dominican Republic, Jamaica, Russia, and Nigeria, as well as ongoing struggles with American gangs and organized crime.

Criticism that the United States is losing the war on drugs notwithstanding, the DEA remains committed to fighting the distribution, sale, and use of illegal drugs. But the battle is getting more expensive in blood, money, agents, and other resources all the time. To fight against the drug lords and their organizations means the DEA must

A Mexican soldier stands guard behind police tape in Ciudad Juarez, Mexico. A number of mass graves were discovered in the building behind him, which was owned by a cartel thought to be responsible for shipping tons of Colombian cocaine across the Rio Grande and into the United States.

continually develop new techniques to engage and defeat an increasingly powerful, sophisticated, and violent enemy who does not play by a fixed set of rules. For the men and women who make up the Drug Enforcement Administration, the effort will have been worth the time and the costs if, in the end, it means returning "America to the drug-free past [it once] enjoyed."

Glossary

Anaesthetic—Painkiller.

Antidepressant—A drug used to relieve or prevent depression.

Cartel—Syndicate or partnership.

Counterculture—A culture with values that run counter to those of established society.

Forfeiture—Losing or giving up property as a result of involvement in a crime.

Hallucinogens—Drugs that produce hallucinations, or perceptions of objects with no reality.

Initiative—Project or campaign.

Interrogate—Interview or question.

Jurisdiction—Authority or control.

Mandatory—Required.

Narcotics—Drugs that dull the senses, reduce pain, or induce sleep.

Prohibition—The forbidding by law of the manufacture, transportation, and sale of alcoholic liquors.

Prosecution—The act of bringing legal action against a criminal or violator of law.

Sedative—A drug tending to calm, moderate, or tranquilize nervousness or excitement.

Smuggling—To import or export something in violation of customs laws.

Surveillance—Close watch kept over someone or something.

Trafficking—Illegal or disreputable commercial activity.

Further Reading

DiLaura, Cynthia, and M. D. Devore. *Kids & Drugs.* New York: Abdo Publishing Company, 1994.

Hicks, John. *"No Way I'm an Addict."* Brookfield, CT: Millbrook Press, 1997.

Kronenwetter, Michael. *Drugs in America: The Users, the Suppliers, the War on Drugs.* New York: Julian Messner, 1990.

McLaughlin, Miriam Smith, and Sandy Pierce Hazorin. *Addiction: The "High" That Brings You Down.* Springfield, NJ: Enslow Press, 1997.

Sprung, Barbara, and Suzanne J. Mordico. *Drug Abuse.* Chatham, NJ: Raintree/Steck-Vaughan, 1998.

Weir, William. *In the Shadow of the Dope Fiend: America's War on Drugs.* New York: Archon, 1997.

DEA website: http://www.usdoj.gov/dea/index.htm

Index

ABOUT THE AUTHOR: Meg Greene earned a bachelor's degree in history at Lindenwood College in St. Charles, Missouri, and master's degrees in history from the University of Nebraska at Omaha and historic preservation from the University of Vermont. Greene is the author of five other books, writes regularly for *Cobblestone* magazine and other publications, and serves as a contributing editor for Suite101.com's "History For Children." She makes her home in Midlothian, Virginia.

SENIOR CONSULTING EDITOR Arthur M. Schlesinger, jr. is the leading American historian of our time. He won the Pulitzer Prize for his book *The Age of Jackson* (1945) and again for *A Thousand Days* (1965). This chronicle of the Kennedy Administration also won a National Book Award. Professor Schlesinger is the Albert Schweitzer Professor of the Humanities at the City University of New York, and he has been involved in several other Chelsea House projects, including the REVOLUTIONARY WAR LEADERS and COLONIAL LEADERS series.

Picture Credits